Manors & Families

of

Derbyshire

Volume Two
M to Z

Series Editor: Peter J. Naylor

ISBN 0 946404 45 3

© 1984

Printed and Published by
J. H. Hall & Sons Limited, Siddals Road, Derby
Printers and Stationers since 1831
Telephone: Derby (0332) 45218

THE DERBYSHIRE HERITAGE SERIES

*'Much it is to be wished
that this princely habitation
may never come so far into
favour as to be modernised'*

Edward King 1782

INTRODUCTION

The English Country House has mostly survived the ravages of war, disease and the weather. It stands as a memorial to those who built it and lived in it. It is often the only survivor of the village of centuries ago, when the great house and the church were of stone. The villagers having to live in more fragile abodes.

These houses have a story to tell, a story of statesmanship, exploration, science, holiness and all the faculties. A book of this size cannot do justice to the whole tale, but it can give a glimpse of an age now gone, when the local squire and land owner looked out onto his many acres, often benevolently.

Derbyshire is rich with such houses, some argue, richer than most other counties. This county has many houses of note, occupied by families that have contributed significantly to the greater knowledge of mankind.

There is room though for the humbler house, the house that once enjoyed a larger degree of authority within the community. Many have been omitted for space limits the choice, and it is acknowledged that certain of the larger houses are not represented in these pages.

The arms will be of interest to those who study heraldry. These are reproduced from 'The Old Halls, Manors and Families of Derbyshire', by 'J. T.' published by C. F. Wardley, Derby, 1892, kindly loaned by Richard Gregory. 'J. T.' was J. Tilley.

A gazetteer is provided which advises the location of the houses and their present use. A surprising number are still in private hands, and access is not permitted except on special occasions.

The sketches within the cartouches are poor, but give an idea of the appearance of the house at the time. The photographs were taken by Steven Antcliffe, Staff Photographer of J. H. Hall & Sons Limited, in the year of publication, 1984, from the same viewpoint as the artist wherever possible. The gazetteer and summaries are by Peter Naylor.

This book is to help the lover of our beautiful country houses to increase his knowledge and awareness of this heritage. To know some of these is to love them. To live in one, as the writer once did, is to know a large and beautiful house in all its varied facets.

There is a new awareness of the need to preserve the larger houses. Let us never again witness the destruction of fine houses such as has been witnessed in Derby of recent years, the reward given by a municipal authority to the generosity of others.

This view of the houses of Derbyshire is, we believe, different in format to other books on the same subject, and consequently answers a need amongst those who love this county. It is in two volumes, alphabetically presented A to L and M to Z respectively for economy of production.

The expression 'Stately Home' has been avoided, an unfortunate name coined in a song. We prefer 'Country House'.

Two of the houses now lie in the City of Sheffield, Totley and Mosbrough. These were ceded by Derbyshire during boundary alterations this century. The spellings used in the script are derived from the current ordnance survey maps and some differ from those used by Tilley. The O.S. spellings are taken as the greater authority. Example: Mosborough - Mosbrough, Winfield - Wingfield, etc.

Crests of the Old Families and Territorial Lords of the Appletree Hundred

Agard No 2	Balguy	Barnesley	Bate	Beaumont	Birde	Blount	Bonell	Bourchur
Bradshaw	Browne	Browne	Butler	Cavendish	Chandos	Clarke	Clifford	Coke
Cox	Colville	Crolton	Crewe	Curzon	Darwin	Dethick	Drury	Every
Eyre	Ferne No 2	Ford				Gerard	Gifford	Gilbert
Greville	Grosvenor	Harpur				Harrison	Nodington	Harwood
Holden	Sodrell	Knivelon	Meynell quartering Meynell, Edensor and Everdon			Lowe	Sawlon	Leche
Longford	Merry	Milward	Mosley	Parr	Payet	Palmer	Pole	Porte
Powtrell	Pye	Rolleston	Roper	Russell	Shaw	Shirley	Reigh	Stanhope
Strutt	Talbot	Turner	Vernon	Wilmot	Wright	Johnson	Meymers	Fitzwilliam

Crests of the Principal Families of the Repton and Moorleston Hundreds

Gould. | Curzon | Donman | Boothby | Byron | Carey
Cecil | Chadwick | | | Dale | Grey.
Armyne | | | | | Borrow
Cavendish | | | | | Chaloner
Cokayne | | Mosley quartering Mosley, Lowe and Tenman | | | Coke.
Shambe | Stant | Babington | Brereton | Corbett | Cotton
Dethfield | Degge. | Ferne | Greensmith | Bassets | Buckley.
Bateman | Buxton. | Gell | Hodge | Fitzherbert. | Meverage.

Crests of the Old Families and Territorial Lords of Wirksworth Wapentake

Hume.	Ireland.	Meynors.	Montgomery.	Ireton.	Munro.
Kirby	Murray	Lascelles.	Newton.	Levenge	Lovel.
Nightengale.	Lascelles	Dawes.	Wall	Hodgkinson	Neville.
Lowe	Manlove	Okeover	Oldfield	Osborne	Mather
Mellor	Molineux	Roper	Pierpoint 1	Pierpoint 2	Rigge
Adderley	Beaufort	Ugard	Bentley	Allestry	Beresford
Alsop	Bingham	Arkwright	Blackwell	Francis	Cooper
Eyre	Evans	Finch	Emmerson	Dawes	Goodwin.

7

Mackworth Quartering Basinges, Normanville, Hercy, Arches, Leke, Somers, Staveley, Talbot, Drayton, Hall, Hopton, Swillington, Barrington, Itchingham.

MACKWORTH CASTLE

8

MACKWORTH CASTLE

What we see today is the gatehouse, built at the turn of the 15th century. Of the castle, if there was one, nothing remains, although a large keep platform was once excavated.

Sir Thomas de Mackworth of the County of Rutland sold the manor to Sir John Curzon in 1655.

Tradition has it that the castle was reduced by Parliamentary forces using cannon fired from the nearby 'Cannon Hills'. Had this been so, one would have expected the gateway to be scarred. It is unmarked by cannon damage and it is devoid of arrow slits. Artifacts have been scarce in the area so one begins to question whether or not a castle was built here.

It has long been the castle that never was. Is this gateway therefore a folly, or did it once guard the entrance to a once great fortification?

The best solution is to assume that a great castle was intended for this site, preparations were duly made, but a shift in strategy caused the builders' to change their minds.

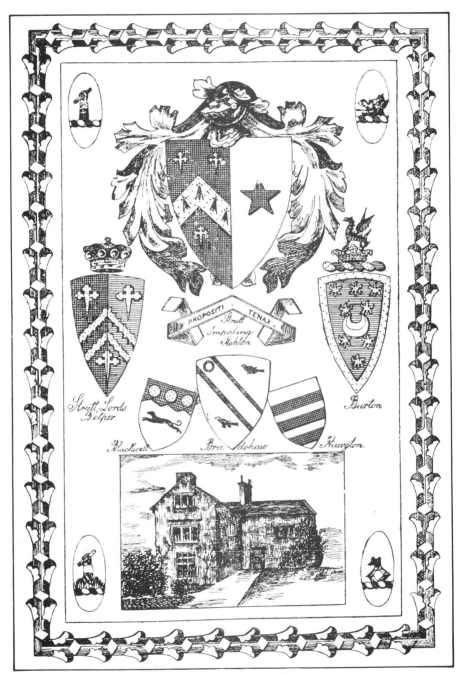

MAKENEY HALL

MAKENEY HALL

Known as Makeney Old Hall and built by 1614. It was repaired and altered in 1893, hence the brick chimneys.

Richard Fletcher built it, but his arms, if he had any, are not represented opposite. It descended through an heiress to the Bradshaws of Duffield, of the adjoining parish. This Bradshaw a son of Anthony, was resplendant in the name of Vicesimus.

George H. Strutt acquired it from the Bradshaws in 1893, who leased it to another, unrelated Fletcher, a tenant farmer.

Duffield church rewards a visit, for here may be seen the monuments of the Bradshaw family, of which Vicesimus was a descendant.

This is yet another house which supposedly sheltered Mary, Queen of Scots.

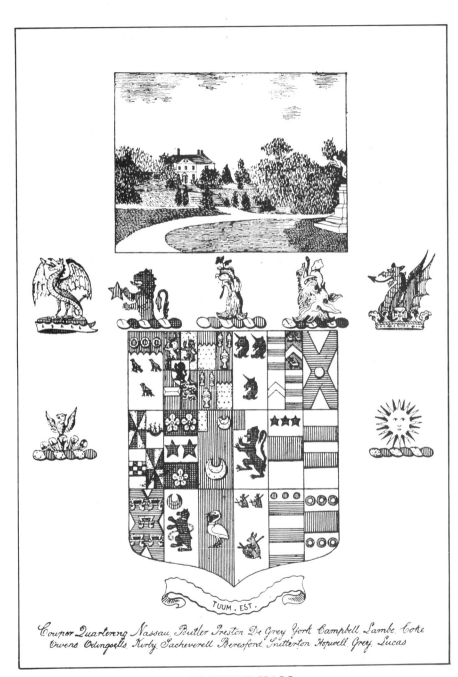

Cowper Quartering Nassau, Butler Preston De Grey York Campbell Lambe Coke Owens Odingsells Kirby Sacheverell Beresford Snitterton Hopwell Grey Lucas

TUUM. EST.

MELBOURNE HALL

MELBOURNE HALL

The original house of the 16th century was a residence for the Bishops of Carlisle, of which some traces remain.

Sir John Coke bought the house in 1630, which family added to it from time to time, with work by Francis Smith, his son William Smith and Gibbs. Sir John was of the Trusley Cokes and was Principal Secretary of State to Charles I.

The house was inherited in 1750 by Sir Matthew Lamb Bt., whose son became Viscount Melbourne, the eminent Prime Minister, after whom the Australian city is named. The Earl Cowper inherited it, and it passed to the Kerrs, Marquis of Lothian in 1905 when the former family became extinct.

The gardens are well worth a visit, the wrought iron arbor by Robert Bakewell is exquisite, and the hundred yards long yew tunnel is unique. An urn remembers Thomas Coke whose gardens these were, and who was Chamberlain to Queen Anne.

The arms opposite predate the Kerrs' arrival, so they are not represented.

The renowned Melbourne Pool in the photograph above reputedly fills the quarry where the stone for Melbourne Castle came from.

COMME · JE · TROUVE ·

Cary Quartering and Spencer, France, England

Sitwell

Wigfall

Stones

Strangeways 2; Darcy, Meinell, Conyers, Percy, Danby

Stuteville

MOSBOROUGH HALL

14

MOSBROUGH HALL

This house commands a very fine position, having views over the Derbyshire countryside. From the roof one can see the towers of seventeen churches.

It stands in the City of Sheffield, but was in the county of Derbyshire until boundary changes placed it elsewhere.

From 1469 the sole owner of the manors of Eckington and Mosbrough was a James Strangeways. These manors remained one until 1660. Mosbrough lies in the parish of Eckington today.

The hall became the seat of the Burtons to 1671, then the residence of Joseph Stone, a merchant, until late in the 18th century. It was then 'modernised' much as one sees it today, by a man named Pearson, a 'Pharmacist of Rotherham'. He was in residence for a few years only and he passed it on to a local family, the Staniforths who lived here until the turn of the century.

It had several tenants to 1843 when the estate was sold to Charles Rotherham for £5,600.

It was derelict for a while until 1975, when it was sold and restored to become a hotel in 1976. It is reputedly haunted.

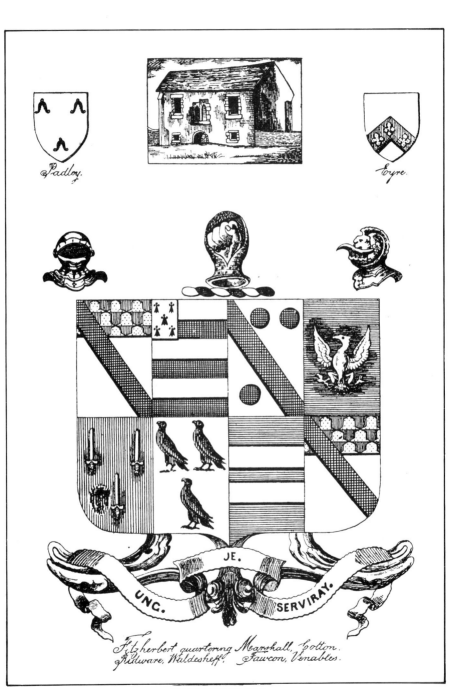

Padley.

Eyre.

UNG. JE. SERVIRAY.

Fitzherbert quartering Marshall, Cotton.
Kidware, Waldeshef. Faucon, Venables.

PADLEY HALL

PADLEY HALL

Of the house known as Padley Manor, (there is a Padley Hall at Ripley), only a remnant survives, for the large 14th century mansion was demolished in 1893 to make way for the adjoining railway.

The building depicted above is now a chapel, although that was not its original use. The manor belonged to the Padleys of Padley, and was inherited by Robert Eyre who built the house. Sir Thomas Fitzherbert married an Eyre heiress, and both were devout catholics, during the anti-catholic hysteria under Elizabeth I.

Two priests took shelter here in 1588, the now famous Nicholas Garlick and Robert Ludlam. They were arrested, 'tried' and died by hanging, drawing and quartering by St. Mary's Bridge, Derby.

One of the Fitzherberts, Thomas died in the Tower in 1591, and John in Fleet Prison seven years later.

In 1933 the Roman Catholic Diocese of Nottingham bought the building and converted it from a cow shed into a chapel.

VESTIGIA. NULLA. RETROSUM.

Kennedy

Sarnes

Tampson

Parkyns

Greene

Cressy

Levinge quartering Corbyn, Greene,
Kennedy, Parkyns, Cressy, Tampson,
Sarnes.

Beresford

Evans

Trott

Segrave

PARWICH HALL

18

PARWICH HALL

A rarity in this part of the county, a house built of brick, with stone quoins. The present one was built by Sir Richard Levinge in 1747, incorporating an earlier 16th century house, having been bought by him from the Cockayne family of Ashbourne.

The Levinges sold it in 1814 to William Evans, thence to distant relatives, the Lewis family. These latter had the gardens laid out by Sir Walter Tapper in 1905.

It stands on a hillside and overlooks the village in a paternalistic way, facing south and sheltered to the north by a hill, like any good house should be.

SOIES · FERME · EN · DIEU.

ESPERANCE

Fitz Walter   De Force   Mowbray   De Lacy

De Vere   De Lacy   De Roos   Albini

Richard   William   Marescal   Mallet
De Clare   De Clare

Fitz Robert   De Bohun

De Vesci   De Quincy

De Fortibus   Mowdfichet

Roger   John of Gaunt   Lanvaley
Bigod

De Hugo   Nardet
Bigod

Huntingfield

F. Clumbe quartering   Loudham, Breton
Fitzwilliam Lucers Dartrain   Clarrell Soresbe Tomine Richards:
Neville Montacute Monthermer Holland Tiptoft   Charlton, Inglethorpe Braddon Delapole Broughe

PEVERIL CASTLE

20

PEVERIL CASTLE

Also known as the 'Castle of the Peak' was built by William Peveril, a natural son and a stalwart of William of Normandy, on a rocky eminence overlooking the village of Castleton and guarding the Valley of the Noe.

The keep, rebuilt by Henry II in 1176 is the largest surviving remnant of this once great fortification, although much curtain walling remains. The keep measures 21 feet by 19 feet, sixty feet high and with walls 8 feet thick.

The Normans also left their mark in the church, which boasts a Norman chancel arch and west tower.

It was at this castle that the same Henry met Malcolm, King of Scotland in 1157, where the latter submitted to the former. The event was celebrated in style for 72 shillings worth of wine was consumed.

The castle is the fanciful setting for Sir Walter Scott's novel, 'Peveril of the Peak'.

Gregson.

Baynall.

Gayer.

Mundy.

Denison.

Stanhope.

Pole Quartering Hartington, Motton, Wakebridge,
Laughton, Chandos, Walkelyn, Twyford, Bradsfort,
Basset Colvile, Boteler, Pantulf, Mallory and
Sacheverell.

RADBOURN HALL

22

RADBOURNE HALL

The Poles, that ancient and well represented family, acquired this estate in the 14th century, and has been in their ownership until today. One of them, German Pole built the house in 1739-54, his architect being Wiliam Smith. The house has work by Joseph Wright, 'Wright of Derby', and Robert Bakewell that prolific metal smith.

The house was tastefully restored in 1958, when the 'Victorianisations', the ruin of many a fine house, were removed.

The foundations of an earlier house, of reputedly enormous proportions, can be seen near to the Radbourne Brook.

A visit to the church is mandatory, for here can be seen the memorials to the Pole family, the oldest being of alabaster, commemorating Peter de la Pole who died in 1432. Those who admire fine wood carving, will find this church to be a treasure house, for Francis Pole had the woodwork brought from Dale Abbey.

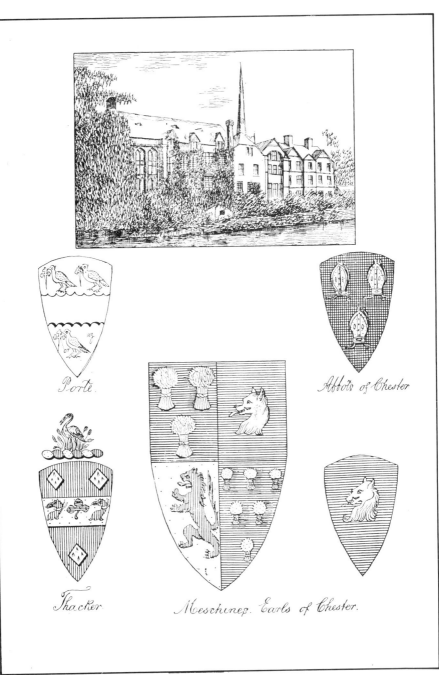

Porte.

Abbots of Chester.

Thacher.

Meschines. Earls of Chester.

REPTON HALL

24

REPTON HALL

The ancient priory of Repton was granted to Thomas Thacker, Steward to Lord Cromwell, at the time of the dissolution. His son Gilbert at the time of Mary Tudor, raised the church to the ground to prevent it being used for worship again. He said at the time that he had, 'destroyed the nest that the birds might not build therein again'.

The Thackers sold part of these ruins to the executors of Sir John Port, who founded the now famous public school here in 1557.

There was trouble between the Thackers and the school, so a house was built to hide in, this is the hall and was for many years the residence of the headmaster of the school. It boasts some fine brickwork, and part of a tower built by Prior John Overton in the 15th century.

Thacker monuments can be seen in the church, including Gilbert's in alabaster and dated 1563.

Badge of the Duke of Lancaster

Badge of the Nevilles

Wolley   Quarlering   Robotham

RIBER HALL

RIBER HALL

Some confuse this with Riber Castle and vice versa. The hall lies snugly in the village, the 'castle' is a hollow ruin on the hilltop.

The hall is 17th century as is the nearby Riber Manor House, and is dated 1661.

Anthony Wooley built the house and died a bachelor in 1668.

It was sold to the Stathams of Tansley, then to the Chappells in 1681 and with the estate was shared between the Greatorex and Walls families in 1724.

The Wooleys were a local family of note, one being an antiquarian who left a priceless collection of local documents to the British Museum. The family lived at nearby Allen Hill, Matlock and their monuments are in Matlock church.

Fosbrooke

Le Hunt.

Holden.

Quartered Arms of Hunt

SHARDLOW HALL

28

SHARDLOW HALL

With Shardlow having been a 'Clapham Junction' of the canal system, we should not be surprised to learn that the Hall has connections with the canals.

The Holdens of Aston sold the estate to the Fosbrookes in the latter half of the 17th century, and these were steeped in the financing and operation of canals.

It was later sold in the 1820's to the Sutton family, who were also involved with the canals. This century, the house was empty for a period until it was acquired for use by the Ministry of Agriculture, Fisheries and Food, who are their still, hence the cars in the picture.

The house is dated 1684 and was greatly altered in 1726. The arms of the Hunts opposite, remind us that the estate belonged to them before the Holdens.

Clifton

Percy

Hickling

Mееринг

Fincens

Stapleton

Bowling Beard

Champion

Bowden q Woodrofe Barnby

Snoks

Browne Impaling Blount

Tegge Quartering Boughey

Bagshawe
With the escutcheon of
Pretence for Ashton.

Lingard.

Mooley

Colville.

Markham.

Jordan.

Minors

Stanton.

Mastneus.

THE RIDGE, MARSH, AND SLACK HALLS

30

SLACK HALL

A Robert Legh owned a large area at 'Slack', an old dialect word for a hollow, witness Slack Hill east of Matlock.

By 1625, a William Lingard owned a hall here, and his family lived there until 1718, when a David Lingard sold it to a Benjamin Bangs of Stockport, who very quickly disposed of it to a Thomas Slack, a name having a happy coincidence, for the house was not named after his family as popularly supposed.

The Lingards were Quakers and suffered for their faith. Some are buried in an old burying ground inside the gates of Ford Hall.

The turnpike cut through the garden of the house, hence the closeness of the highway to the house.

Adderley.

Ferne

Turner.

Shore.

Milward.

Shirley.

BONNE.

EN.

FOY.

*Sacheverell. quartering Snitterton. Fitz-Ereald
Stalham, Massey Risley. Morley, De la Laund, Trelaferen.*

SNITTERTON HALL

32

SNITTERTON HALL

A fine and attractive Derbyshire house, of pleasing proportions and having good mullioned windows.

Built in 1631 by John Milward, of the Eaton Dovedale Milwards, it had several owners subsequently, as has the medieval moated house that predated this one.

The Snittertons were the first here, the Sacheverells inheriting the site in the 15th century. They sold it to John Shore of Darley in 1596, who disposed of it to the Smiths of Padley Hall. Four years later, in 1631, Milward bought it, to be inherited by Charles Adderley, who promptly sold it to Henry Ferne of Parwich in 1695, to be inherited by the Turners. Colonel B. G. Davie bought the house in 1908, who sold it to the then tenants, the Bagshawes of Ford, who still live here. Colonel Davie married into an old local family, changing his name to Davie-Thornhill.

A monument to Henry Ferne can be seen in Bonsall Church.

Bingham

Brownlow.

Chappell

Giffard quartering Giffard (ancient), Montgomery,
Montgomery (ancient), Stafford, Francis.

PRENEZ HALEINE, TIREZ FORT.

Harbord.

Harwood.

Hodge

SOMERSALL MANOR HOUSE

SOMERSAL MANOR HOUSE

This is Somersal Herbert Hall, an unspoiled and superb example of a timber framed house.

John Fitzherbert built it in 1564, the south west front being built of brick and the porch being added in 1899. John and his wife Ellen are remembered by two wooden tables in the porch, dated 1564, which must be joined and matched to enable an inscription to be deciphered.

Lord Vernon of Sudbury bought it in 1803 and resold it to Lord St. Helens, the Tissington branch of the Fitzherberts. Mr. J. V. Green, a Derby tape manufacturer bought it in 1956.

The house can boast being unspoiled both inside and out, unaffected by 'improvements' and is therefore a unique example of a house of the period.

Barlow

Bridgeman.

Cavendish quartering Scudamore, Smith, Brielknock, Hardwick, Pinchbeck, Ogle, Neville, Chartney, Golson, Healon, Alton, Bertram, Kirby, Varnaby, Halton, Basset, Bussey, Bradford, Inford, Rolle, Dethick, Meohyt, Stafford, Meignell, Savage, Meynell, De Verdon, Verdon, Byron, Harnslor Colnot, Clayfar.

STOKE HALL

STOKE HALL

Lord Grey of Codnor Castle sold the estate in 1473 to Robert Barlow, who sold it to Bess of Hardwick in 1581, thence by descent it came into the possession of the Earl of Newcastle.

Jacinth Sacheverell of Morley bought it in 1656, it being inherited by the father of the builder of the present house, the Reverend John Simpson in 1757.

Soon after, it was inherited by Henry Bridgeman, 5th Earl of Bradford, one of whose sons took the name of Simpson.

It was tenanted throughout the present century and has been recently sold. It was reputedly designed by William Booth of Stoney Middleton and Thorold suggests that James Paine had a hand in it. It should be mentioned that Booth was an avid student of Paines' works.

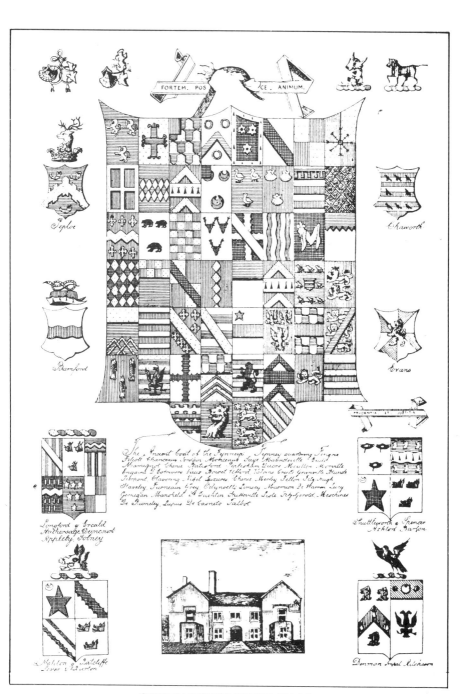

STONY MIDDLETON HALL

STONEY MIDDLETON HALL

The house is 17th century, altered and enlarged 200 years later, the interior being spoiled by Victorianisation.

It was long the home of the Denmans, one Joseph Denman of Bakewell, was the uncle of Thomas who was an eminent judge and who constantly tried to have slavery abolished. He was Lord Chief Justice in 1832 and he defended Queen Caroline at her trial. It is this Denman who gave his name to so many hotels, for he was a popular hero of his day, for his advocacy on behalf of the queen.

One of his sons became an admiral, the other a judge. Thomas kept black pigs and lived to be 89.

Lord Denman built the bath house over a nearby spring, the site of a Roman bath. The water overflows into a stream, which flows through the gardens of an estate of houses, once part of the grounds of the hall.

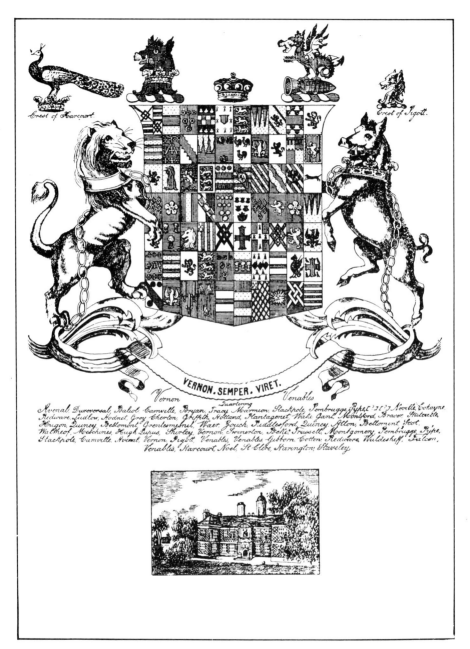

Crest of Harcourt

Crest of Jigott

VERNON. SEMPER. VIRET.

Vernon   Quartering   Venables

Avenal, Durevoxsal, Baliol, Camville, Bryan, Tracy, Marmion, Stackpole, Pembrugge, Pype, 1E.J Novill, Cokayne, Redware, Ludlow, Hodnet, Grey, Cherlton, Griffith, Holland, Plantagenet, Wake, Janl, Mountford, Bracer, Stuteville, Hougon, Quincey, Bellomont, Grenteximesnil, Waer, Gouch, Puddlesford, Quincey, Allon, Bellomont, Feot. Walkeof, Meschines, Hugh Lupus, Shirley, Vernon, Ironerton, Belle, Trussell, Montgomery, Pembrugge, Pype, Stackpole, Camville, Avenal, Vernon, Jigott, Venables, Venables-Gibbom, Cotton, Redware, Wuldeshelf, Falcon, Venables, Harcourt, Noel, St. Clere, Harington, Staveley.

SUDBURY HALL

SUDBURY HALL

Another jewel in the crown of Derbyshire, for whilst it is now largely bare of furniture, it boasts superb plasterwork by Bradbury and Pettifer, an overmantle by Grinling Gibbons and a Great Stair carved by Edward Pierce.

The house has an atmosphere of tranquility and intimacy, rare in a building of this size.

It was built by George Vernon, acting as his own architect, in the 17th century. His wealth was acquired from a series of astute marriages. This Vernon was a branch of the Vernons of Haddon, and his descendant lives next door.

The servants' wing was added 1876-83, and now houses a Museum of Childhood. The gardens are disappointing, the lake in contrast is attractive. The folly to the north is an eye catcher and deer cote built in the 1700s, an echo of the days when it was part of a park and an estate of 6,000 acres.

The writer once had the privilige of calling this house his home.

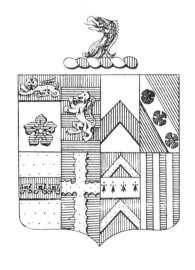

Rolleston quartering Wakelyn, Stafford,
Winfield, Bringham, Chatnells, Wollaton, Strelley.

Harper 1894

Harper 1894.

SWARKESTON HALL

42

SWARKESTONE HALL

This house forms part of the Harpur-Crewe Estate and is tenanted by a farmer.

An earlier house dating from the 16th century, and occupied by the Harpurs is demolished, and could have been quarried for the building of Calke Abbey.

Prior to the Harpurs, the Findernes occupied the site.

Parts of the garden walling may have been part of the original house, the present one dates from the 17th century.

The 'grandstand' nearby and within the grounds of the hall was erected in 1632 and is reputed to have been used by spectators at jousting fairs. It makes a pleasant eye catcher. It overlooks an area called the bowling green or balcony field.

Sir Richard Harpur, whose home was here, was one of Queen Elizabeth's judges, and Justice of the Common Pleas.

Colonel Hastings fortified the earlier house for the king in 1643, for this is a strategic place, close by the meandering Trent. It was here in December, 1745 that Bonnie Prince Charlie's Highland Army reached its most southerly point. After holding the bridge for two nights he retreated to whence he came. A Colonel Hastings did see battle, for he was dislodged by Sir John Gell of Hopton, a staunch Parliamentarian, in January 1643.

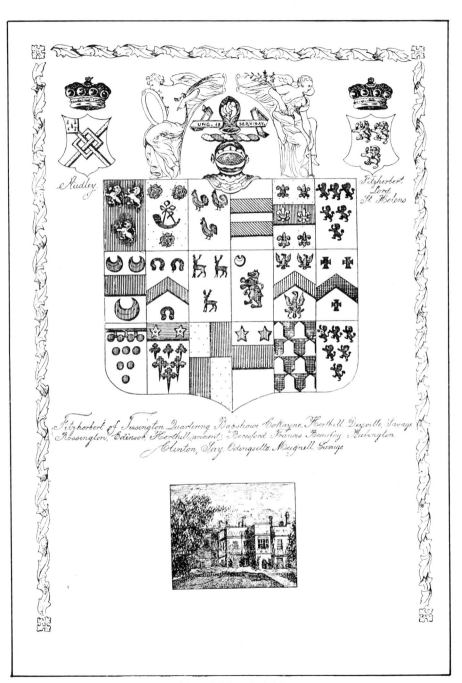

Audley

Fitzherbert Lord St Helens

UNG. JE SERVIRAY

Fitzherbert of Tissington Quartering Bagshawe CoKayne Herthill Deyvile Savage Rossington, Edinsor, Herthill, ancient, Beresford Francis Beaufoy Babington Clinton, Say, Odingselts Meignell Savage

TISSINGTON HALL

44

TISSINGTON HALL

What can be said to give justice to this house and village. It is every American's dream of an English village, yet it is a Derbyshire village in appearance and character.

Francis Fitzherbert built this house in 1609, but the family had been here for a hundred years, it being previously the property of the Clintons, Meynells, Savages and Francis, whose heiress married a Fitzherbert. The baronetcy was granted in 1783, by King George III to Sir William Fitzherbert, in recognition of his services as Gentleman Usher.

Alleyne, the younger brother of Sir William became Baron St. Helens, for his services as a diplomat to the Russian court.

The Reverend Richard Graves wrote 'The Spiritual Quixote' here in 1745, the year of the Jacobite Rebellion, and a Fitzherbert is featured in the novel as Sir William Forester of whom it was said, 'He had the art of making every company happy, and the greater art of making himself happy in every company'.

The garden gate is yet another of Robert Bakewell's works, and the garden front was remodelled in the 18th century. The house is Jacobian and not Elizabethan as sometimes stated.

A Fitzherbert lives here still.

Willoughby

SANS.

VERITE. PEUR.

Milner Quartering Walton

Wortley

Leche

TOTLEY HALL

46

TOTLEY HALL

As with Mosbrough Hall, Totley was once in the county of Derbyshire, now placed in Sheffield due to boundary changes, in 1935.

The old house above, replaced an earlier one which was demolished.

The coat of arms, with the date of 1623 and the initials GN, tell us when the present hall was built and who by, George Newbold. He was of the Newbolds of Unstone near Chesterfield.

The large addition to the right of the old house, of which the picture shows a small slice, was built in 1883.

A deed of 1407 shows that the manor had been in the hands of the Milnes of Aslockton in Nottinghamshire, who were related to the Cokes. These were the Cokes of Trusley having links with the Viscounts Melbourne and the Earls Cowper.

It was acquired by Sheffield Corporation for educational purposes in 1944. The hall is now overshadowed by the new buildings of Totley College, many of which were built in the period 1950-3.

Kyrke, Quartering
Vernon Lushington

Kyrke.

UT. TIBI.   ALTERI.

SIC.

Bowles Quartering Bradshaw Stafford Rowland Very Frances Gulliard Kinsley
& Wakefield

WHITEHOUGH AND BRADSHAW HALLS

WHITEHOUGH HALL

Whitehough or Whitehalgh was once the name for an area of land on Bradshaw Edge. Ownership is difficult to trace due to numerous sales and boundary changes.

In 1433, a Ralph Kirke was demandant in a fine relating to Whitehalgh, and a Hugh Kirke appears in 1454 and 1471 in connection with the property. Several names crop up in connection with the house, the Kirk's, the Moults and the Glossops.

On the death of Samuel Kirke in 1765, a long tenure indeed, the house and estate passed to his son in law, the Reverend William Plumbe, Rector of Aughton.. His two daughters inherited the estate, broke it up and sold it in 1806. The hall was bought by a John Booth, who built a paper mill on some of the land, naming it Whitehall Mill.

It is now the Old Hall Inn.

Munro

Rivett

Hope

Statham
Quartering Wigley, Denham,
Meverell, Daniel, Gaylton

Boscherville

Bec

Mackenzie

Withipole

Mather

ADJUTATOR · MEUS · DEUS ·

WIGWELL GRANGE

50

WIGWELL GRANGE

Wigwell was a monastic grange associated with Darley Abbey, the estate having been given to the Prior and Canons of St. Mary at about the year 1200. It was reputed to be the favourite summer residence of the Abbots.

All of this is now gone, except that there is evidence of the original grange in the cellars, and the fish stews can be made out nearby.

After the dissolution, the estate was sold to Henry Wigley of Middleton-by-Wirksworth. The Wigleys retained the estate until 1700, when it passed by marriage to Sir John Statham of Tideswell, the last person to be knighted by Queen Anne in 1714.

The line died out, and after a period during which it was unoccupied, the Hobsons tenanted the house.

The estate was sold to a John Mander of Bakewell, who resold it in 1774 to a Francis Green. Francis Green Goodwin inherited it, and it passed to his descendant William Henry Goodwin, who died in 1877.

It has had a precarious existance since that date and has been sold recently.

Leacroft

Halton

Howard

SOLA · VIRTUS · INVICTA

Cromwell

Talbot

WINFIELD MANOR HOUSE

52

WINGFIELD MANOR

Mary, Queen of Scots did stay here, for she was an unwilling prisoner of Elizabeth in 1569 and 1584, her jailer being the owner, the 6th Earl of Shrewsbury, husband of Bess of Hardwick. Stories of tunnels from here to other houses, such as Heage Hall can be safely discounted. What must be credited is the size of the house, measuring 416 feet by 256 feet overall.

It is now in ruins, another victim of the Civil War, being reduced by Sir John Gell of Hopton, again. It was lived in after the war by the Halton family, who quarried the ruin to build Wingfield Hall nearby. Ralph, Lord Cromwell, Warden of Sherwood Forest, Constable of Nottingham Castle, Lord Treasurer of England started to build the manor on a moated site in the 1440s. Part of the latter can be seen today.

It passed by marriage to the Howards, the Dukes of Norfolk who passed it on to Immanuel Halton, an astronomer and the Duke's steward. The Haltons left the manor for the hall in 1774. It lay ruinous for about a century, when it was taken over as a farm, its present use.

It was here that the Babington Plot was hatched to rescue Mary. Babington lost his head for his attempt in 1586.

It is an attractive ruin, now being painstakingly preserved. The ghost of Mary is here still in this beautiful corner of Derbyshire.

A far cry from Gell's 'Sanctuary of all the papists and delinquents of that county'.

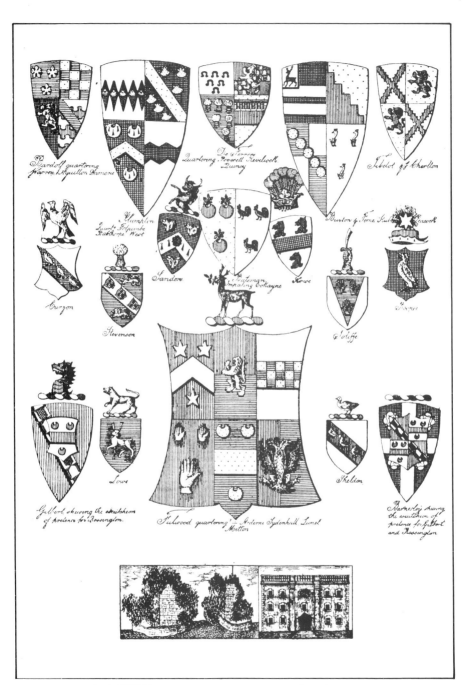

WINSTER HALL AND MIDDLETON CASTLE

54

WINSTER HALL

This hall comes as a surprise, it is grand in a small way, for it sits in a village of simple hillside cottages.

It dates from the middle of the 18th century. An earlier house stood here, dating from the time of James I, and built by Francis Moore, a lead merchant. His descendant built the present house, one George Moore. A memorial to the once prosperous local industry of lead mining, for Winster is an old mining village of importance. James Norman acquired it by marrying George's daughter and it passed into the Carill-Worsley family by marriage.

For a time it was the home of Llewellyn Jewitt, the antiquary, who was also a skilled engraver, and author on many subjects.

The hall has fine pillasters and a balustraded parapet, built of stone conveyed or 'jagged' from the quarries at nearby Darley Dale, the same stone that was used for the Thames Embankment.

Folgambe.

Eyre.

De Ferrars.

Plumpton.

FORMA. FLOS. FAMA. FLATUS.

Bagshawe quartering Gill, Westby and Drake.

WORMHILL HALL

WORMHILL HALL

The 17th century hall is associated with the Bagshaws of Ford, who also held the living at Wormhill Church up to the turn of the century. One of these Bagshaws was William, the Apostle of the Peak. However, the Bagshaws could be less grand, for Nicholas was made clerk and schoolmaster in 1674, 'for want of a better'.

The Reverend William, when returning from Castleton recorded, "I was sorry to observe a party of boys playing football. I spoke to them but was laughed at, and on my departure one of the boys gave the ball a wonderful kick — a proof of the degeneracy of human nature". What would he have to say of 20th century boys?

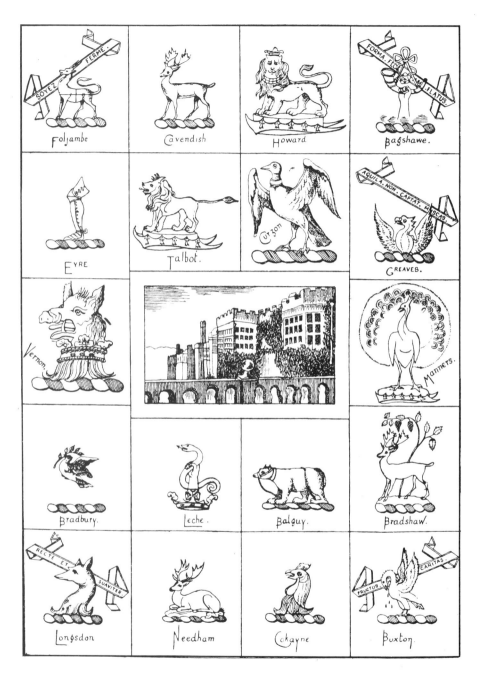

CRESTS OF THE OLD PEAK FAMILIES

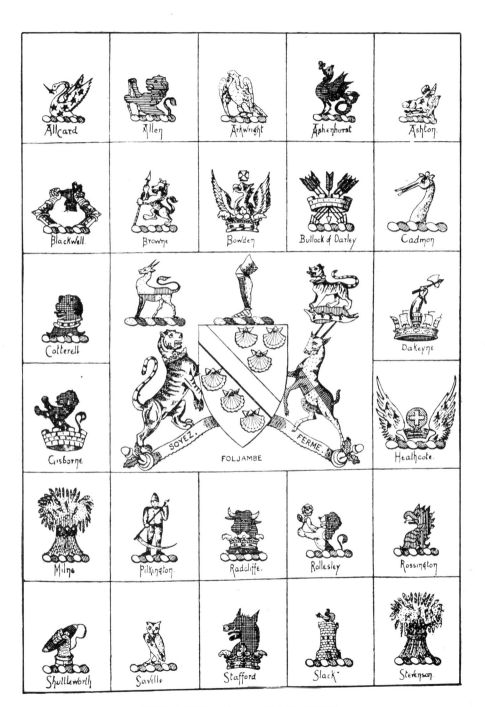

CRESTS OF THE OLD PEAK FAMILIES

CRESTS OF THE OLD PEAK FAMILIES